North American
Animals

ARMADILLOS

by Steve Potts

Consulting Editor: Gail Saunders-Smith, PhD

CAPSTONE PRESS
a capstone imprint

Pebble Plus is published by Capstone Press,
1710 Roe Crest Drive, North Mankato, Minnesota 56003.
www.capstonepub.com

Books published by Capstone Press are manufactured with paper
containing at least 10 percent post-consumer waste.

Library of Congress Cataloging-in-Publication Data
Potts, Steve, –
    Armadillos / by Steve Potts.
        p. cm.—(Pebble plus. North American animals)
    Includes bibliographical references and index.
    Summary: "Simple text and full-color photographs provide a brief introduction to armadillos"—Provided by publisher.
    ISBN 978-1-4296-7704-2 (library binding)
    ISBN 978-1-4296-7921-3 (paperback)
    1. Armadillos—Juvenile literature. I. Title. II. Series.
    QL737.E23P685 2012
    599.3'12—dc23   2011025652

Editorial Credits
Erika L. Shores, editor; Heidi Thompson, designer; Svetlana Zhurkin, media researcher;
    Kathy McColley, production specialist

Photo Credits
Corbis: All Canada Photos/Stephen J. Krasemann, 7, All Canada Photos/Wayne Lynch, 5; Dreamstime: Mike Brown,
cover; iStockphoto: jfc215, 10–11, Lisa Kyle Young, 8–9, 15; National Geographic Stock: Bianca Lavies, 16–17, 21;
Nature Picture Library: Paula Coulter, 19; Shutterstock: Bonnie Fink, 13, mlorenz, 1

Note to Parents and Teachers

The North American Animals series supports national science standards related to life
science. This book describes and illustrates armadillos. The images support early readers in
understanding the text. The repetition of words and phrases helps early readers learn new
words. This book also introduces early readers to subject-specific vocabulary words, which are
defined in the Glossary section. Early readers may need assistance to read some words and to
use the Table of Contents, Glossary, Read More, Internet Sites, and Index sections of the book.

Printed in the United States of America in North Mankato, Minnesota.
102011   006405CGS12

Table of Contents

Living in North America 4

Up Close! 8

Eating 12

Growing Up 16

Staying Safe 20

Glossary 22

Read More 23

Internet Sites 23

Index 24

Living in North America

Armadillos are shy, nocturnal animals. Many kinds of armadillos live in South America. Only the nine-banded armadillo is found in North America.

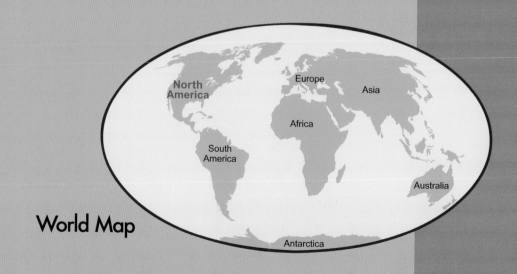

World Map

Armadillos live in the southern
United States and Central America.
They dig burrows in sandy soil
near streams or ponds. Burrows keep
armadillos cool during the day.

North America Map

where armadillos live

Up Close!

Armadillos are about the size of a large cat. They weigh 9 to 16 pounds (4 to 7 kilograms). Armadillos have small heads and long snouts.

Armadillos have a thick outer
skin called a carapace.
The nine-banded armadillo
gets its name from the bands
circling its carapace.

Eating

Armadillos eat both

plants and insects.

They mostly eat beetles.

But they also eat ants, termites,

spiders, berries, and roots.

Armadillos sniff out food in the ground. Their claws dig into the soil. Then their long, sticky tongues snatch up to 60 insects at once.

Growing Up

Armadillos mate between June and September. Eight months later, a female gives birth to four pups. They live in a nest of grass and leaves.

Newborn pups have soft, pink skin. Within days, their carapaces begin to harden and turn brown or gray. Pups leave the nest after three months.

Staying Safe

When scared, armadillos jump

in the air, then run away.

Cars often hit jumping armadillos.

Armadillos that stay safe live

up to 10 years.

Glossary

burrow—a tunnel or hole in the ground made or used by an animal

carapace—the thick, protective shell that covers most of an armadillo

mate—to join together to produce young

nocturnal—active at night and resting during the day

snout—the long front part of an animal's head; it includes the nose, mouth, and jaws

Read More

Jango-Cohen, Judith. *Let's Look at Armadillos*. Animal Close-Ups. Minneapolis: Lerner Publications, 2011.

Schuetz, Kari. *Armadillos*. Backyard Wildlife. Minneapolis: Bellwether Media, 2012.

Sebastian, Emily. *Armadillos*. Animals Underground. New York: PowerKids Press, 2012.

Internet Sites

FactHound offers a safe, fun way to find Internet sites related to this book. All of the sites on FactHound have been researched by our staff.

Here's all you do:

Visit *www.facthound.com*

Type in this code: 9781429677042

Check out projects, games and lots more at
www.capstonekids.com

Index

burrows, 6

carapaces, 10, 18

cars, 20

claws, 14

food, 12, 14

jumping, 20

life span, 20

mating, 16

nests, 16, 18

nocturnal, 4

pups, 16, 18

size, 8

skin, 10

snouts, 8

tongues, 14

Word Count: 215

Grade: 1

Early-Intervention Level: 19